1... 2... COOK!

Quick & Easy Meals for One or Two People

Don Alexander

© 2002 by Don Alexander. All rights reserved.

No part of this book may be reproduced, stored in a retrieval system, or transmitted by any means, electronic, mechanical, photocopying, recording, or otherwise, without written permission from the author.

ISBN: 1-4033-5709-9 (e-book)
ISBN: 1-4033-5710-2 (Paperback)
ISBN: 1-4033-5711-0 (Hardcover)

This book is printed on acid free paper.

1stBooks - rev. 10/08/02

Table of Contents

INTRODUCTION.. VII

CHAPTER ONE
WHO SHOULD READ THIS BOOK?....................................... 1

CHAPTER TWO
THE BARE ESSENTIALS 5

CHAPTER THREE
GETTING STARTED.. 11

CHAPTER FOUR
PASTA DISHES 15

CHAPTER FIVE
RICE DISHES... 23

CHAPTER SIX
MEAT DISHES... 29

CHAPTER SEVEN
CHICKEN DISHES.. 43

CHAPTER EIGHT
PORK DISHES 59

CHAPTER NINE
FISH DISHES 67

CHAPTER TEN
DINNERS FOR THAT SPECIAL PERSON 75

CHAPTER ELEVEN
SIDE DISHES AND SAUCES 87

iv

Acknowledgements

I would never have been able to write this book without the inspiration and help of two people. I would first like to thank my mom for letting me watch her cook when I was a child, and for teaching me how to cook. Without you I wouldn't know how to cook in the first place. I would also like to thank my girlfriend Carrie O'Brien for all the love and support you have given me though this whole process, inspiring me to finish the book, and for testing out the recipes and taking some of the pictures of the completed dishes. I truly appreciate everything you have done for me.

Introduction

viii

From as early as I can remember, I have enjoyed cooking. When I was a kid back home in Indiana, I loved to hang out in the kitchen and watch my mom cook. For some reason it fascinated me to watch my mom with all those pots and pans, chopping and slicing food, and somehow timing everything perfectly so that all the dishes were done at the same time. For a child, this seemed amazing. For an adult, this was quite an accomplishment.

I wondered how my mom knew when to start cooking each dish to get them to finish cooking all at the same time. I know that most children didn't think about things like this. They just wanted to know when dinner was going to be done, but I really did have a fascination with the whole cooking process.

There were five children and two adults in our house when I was growing up. I had three brothers and one sister. Those of you with big families know that dinner is more like an event than a meal. With four boys in the house, my mom cooked meals that could be likened to a mini-Thanksgiving dinner every night. While I was growing up, we didn't order out or go out to dinner very much. My mom cooked dinner almost every night. She always made everything from scratch, and always made a lot of it. Having four boys in the house meant a lot of cooking, and usually little leftovers.

I think what got me hooked on cooking was the first time my mom let me help out with dinner. It started out as one of those days when I was watching my mom cook. I had watched her cook many times, but today was different. That day, my mom asked me if I wanted to help. "Heck, yes!" I thought. She let me stir one of the pots on the stove. I can't remember what it was that I stirred. It was probably corn, beans, or something that really didn't need much attention. I stirred that pot like it was the most fragile dish that needed my undivided attention. I now know that my mom didn't need any help making dinner, but that day I felt like I had made dinner. From that day forward, I knew that I loved to cook. I became mom's little helper in the kitchen. As I got older, I helped out more and more, from chopping up vegetables, to actually preparing some of the dishes for dinner.

I never knew how handy this talent would become until after I got out of college and moved into my first apartment. For the first few months of living on my own, dinner consisted of whatever hot hors d'oeuvres the local bars were serving during happy hour. This became my way of getting a hot meal for dinner almost every night of the week. On weekends, I would go home to visit my parents who lived an hour away. My mom still cooked extravagant dinners, which I gladly devoured. If there were any leftovers, I took them home with me, and heated them up the next day in the microwave. I occasionally cooked for myself, but the happy hours were convenient, and gave me the opportunity to socialize with my friends.

After putting on 20 pounds from all the pizza and deep-fried hors d'oeuvres, I decided that I should start eating healthier. I figured out that my most unhealthy meal of the day was dinner (if you wanted to call it that). So, I broke down and started making my own dinners. At first, it was either pasta this, or chicken that. I didn't know many recipes. I remembered some of the things that I had learned from watching my mom cook, but all of those recipes made dinners big enough to feed an army. I didn't know how to cook for one person. I started watching cooking shows on TV and tried some of the dishes I learned by watching those shows. You single people out there know that when you are bored, you'll watch practically anything on TV.

I stopped going to happy hours for dinner, and started to cook dinner for myself. I tried a few of the dishes I learned on TV, with good results. Dinnertime had switched from getting in line at the bar to fight for the scraps of pizza left on the table, and praying that they were going to bring out a fresh pizza soon, to cooking my own dinner. I enjoyed these dinners while sitting in my Lazy Boy watching TV. The more cooking shows I watched, the more recipes I had for dinner. I soon learned enough recipes that I didn't have to eat the same dinner twice in a week. I started coming up with variations of the recipes I learned from TV cooking shows, and before long, I could just look in the refrigerator and whip something up.

Cooking for myself had many benefits. I found out after a few months that it was healthier for me to make my own dinners instead of eating out every night. I started to lose the twenty pounds I had gained from the nightly happy hour grease fests. I'm not saying that everything I made was supper healthy, but it was sure healthier than consuming half a bottle of Crisco oil in deep fried bar food each night.

I also found out that cooking was good for other things. It was a great stress reliever for me. When I would get home, I was usually starving and stressed out from work. The first thing I did when I walked in the door was think about what I was going to cook for dinner. This instantly got my mind off of work. If I had a bad day at work, I would make a dinner that required more preparation. Chopping up meat and vegetables was a stress reliever. Better to chop up some vegetables than to chop up my computer! One problem I kept encountering was all the recipes I knew made enough food for 4 to 6 people. That's what gave me the idea for this book.

xii

Quick and Easy Meals for One or Two People

Chapter One

Who Should Read This Book?

Don Alexander

Quick and Easy Meals for One or Two People

This book is intended for the single person, or couples, who are not of a culinary nature, and want to make dinners for one or two people. To put it bluntly, if you can't cook, this book is for you. It's tough enough cooking for an entire family. Cooking for only one or two people presents its own slew of challenges. When you cook for just one or two people, you have to take a slightly different approach to the things you make, and how much you make of it. When you make enough food to feed an army, but only one person, or maybe two, sits down to dinner, you are going to have a lot of leftovers. I think that we all know that leftovers equal wasted money. There are only so many days in a row that you can eat the same thing. For me, leftovers presented another problem. Most of the time I would forget about the leftovers, and I was not the kind of person that cleaned out the fridge every week. So after a few weeks, the inside of my fridge looked more like a collection of high school science experiments gone wrong than leftovers.

The cooking shows that I watched gave me great ideas of things to make, but there was still one problem. These recipes usually made enough food for 4 or more people. I still hadn't found any recipes that were for one or two people. That is why I decided to write this book. Let's face it. Our generation is not known for their culinary nature. We are busy people. We don't have a lot of time to cook large meals, but deep down we all still enjoy a home cooked meal. Most of us think that Boston Market is our only way of getting anything close to a home cooked meal nowadays.

If your idea of a home cooked meal is making yourself a peanut butter and jelly sandwich, or boiling water for macaroni and cheese, then you really need this book. Now, when I say that I am going to help teach you how to cook, I mean cooking a hot meal that may actually cover at least two of the 4 basic food groups.

There is even a chapter in this book with great meals you can cook for that special person. Guys, women love it when you cook for them. And ladies, you all know that the way to a man's heart is through his stomach. It also has some good side dishes and sauces that compliment the main courses. So whether it is for survival, parties, or it is to impress a date, cooking comes in pretty handy.

Don Alexander

Another reason I wanted to write this book is because I've always wished that someone had written a book like this about 8 years ago when I really needed it the most. I've seen cookbooks that have quick and easy recipes in them. Many of the recipes were good, but I just wish that someone wrote a cookbook from the single person's or couples perspective where the recipes were designed for one or two people. So I hope this book will give you some good ideas on quick and easy recipes. I hope you enjoy the book, and happy cooking!

Quick and Easy Meals for One or Two People

Chapter Two

The Bare Essentials

Don Alexander

Quick and Easy Meals for One or Two People

We are getting close to actually having you start cooking. The first thing we need to do is go grocery shopping. Last time I checked, groceries do not just magically appear in your refrigerator. What a beautiful thing it would be if they did! All of the recipes have a list of ingredients that you need to make each dish; however, there are a few items that I have found to be bare essentials for anyone to make good tasting food.

Generally speaking, when a person who can't really cook thinks of cooking, the one thing that often gets overlooked is seasoning. I'm not just talking about salt and pepper, although salt and pepper are crucial to cooking. I am talking about the different spices that give a meal its distinction. You are probably thinking, okay, here it is. This is where it gets really complicated and expensive. Don't worry. These are spices that are cheap, can be used in a lot of different meals, and don't have weird names to remember.

The next time you go shopping, pick up the following spices: Onion Powder, Garlic Powder, Oregano, Parsley Flakes, Salt, Pepper, Lemon Pepper Seasoning (this is a pretty good one), Worchestishire Sauce (okay, one of them has a weird name), Soy Sauce, Parmesan Cheese, Bay Leaves, Thyme and Dill.

I know that it sounds like a lot, and that spices can be expensive. Don't worry. All of these spices come in the store brands in the larger containers. This will make them cheaper, and last a lot longer. Trust me, you wont have to buy spices again for a long time if you by these in the large containers. These spices are probably the most widely used spices in preparing quick and easy meals.

Besides the spices, there are a few, okay, several other items that can be bought ahead of time and stored for whenever you need them. These things store for a long time, so they won't go spoil quickly, and you won't be wasting money. I found that having the following items on hand really helped me out of jams when I wanted to make some quick and easy meals. Some of these items can also be used to make some pretty extravagant meals. Since you are already going to the store to get the spices, you might as well pick the following things:

A box of Jiffy baking mix. This one is crucial. There are so many things you can make with this stuff you won't believe it. This stuff is

Don Alexander

also great for breakfast on the weekends if you graduate to the next level, and like cooking enough to start cooking breakfast on the weekends. The breakfast thing also comes in handy in the dating department, but we'll cover that one later. The Jiffy baking mix also has some easy recipes on the back of the box that you can use for dinner.

A box of frozen boneless, skinless chicken breasts. If you are going to make things fast and easy, you don't want to sit there and hack up a whole chicken just to get one dinner out of it. These come individually wrapped, so if you want just one, you can just thaw out one. They also thaw out quickly in the package in some cool water.

Cans of Red Gold chopped tomatoes. They have some with Italian seasoning and some with jalapenos in them (if you like things spicy). These are great because it saves you the time of chopping tomatoes. The seasoned ones save you the trouble of having to do a lot of seasoning. You'll find out that a lot of quick and easy dishes that can be made with diced tomatoes.

Packages of ground beef or ground turkey. I can never keep enough packages of these around. They freeze and store easily in aluminum foil and keep for a long time. Most of the time the packages come in approximately 1 lb. packages. It might be easier divide them and store them as ½ lb. packages. Most of the time you won't need more than ¼ or ½ a pound of ground meat for the meals.

A package of elbow macaroni. This is for some pasta dishes in the book. This will keep for a long time.

A package of mostacolli noodles. Same as the elbow macaroni, this will keep for a long time.

A package of rotini noodles. Same as the elbow macaroni, this will keep for a long time.

A package of frozen white fish. This will keep for awhile, and will come in handy for a meal or two in the book.

Quick and Easy Meals for One or Two People

A couple of jars of your favorite pasta sauce. These will stay fresh until you open them. Then you have to refrigerate them. So you should probably buy the small to medium size jars, unless you plan to make a couple of meals that have pasta sauce in them in the same week.

A bag of rice. How big? It depends on how much you like rice. I eat a lot of it, so I get the 3 lb. bag. Some of the dishes call for rice. If you like rice a lot, you can always boil up extra and eat it with other meals. The key to re-heating rice is to microwave it with a little bit of water. Rice tends to dry out in the refrigerator.

Once you have stocked up with these things, you should only have to buy the miscellaneous stuff when you go to the store, milk, cheese, eggs, yadda, yadda, yadda. You should only have to replenish the items above once in a blue moon.

You will have a larger than normal grocery bill the first time you go to the store after reading this book. Don't worry. All the trips to the store won't be like this. After awhile you will find that you are actually saving money. All those pizzas and take out food can get pretty expensive.

Don Alexander

Quick and Easy Meals for One or Two People

Chapter Three

Getting Started

Don Alexander

Quick and Easy Meals for One or Two People

The rest of the book is made up of basic dinner dishes that are pretty simple to make and may give you some leftovers to take to work for lunch the next day. That is, of course, unless you eat as much as I do. If you do eat as much as I do, then these recipes should be just enough for dinner. These are dishes that shouldn't take much preparation, and shouldn't take too long to make. I know that after a long day of work, the last thing that anyone wants to do is to be cooking for an hour to get a good hot meal.

By the way, I like meat, so many of the recipes in this book contain some sort of meat. If you are a vegetarian, many of these recipes can be made without the meat.

The one thing you will notice is that I don't give you measurements for the spices on some of the dishes. Cooking is not like baking. There is no real set recipe to all dishes. When it comes to spices, I like to taste as I go. I taste the food. If I think that it needs more salt, I'll put more salt in it. The recipes have the spices listed, but I will usually use the terms dash and pinch for the amounts. If you like more spices in your food, then by all means put more in. Make sure you taste as you go. That way you have an idea of how it is going to taste and if it needs more seasoning before you sit down to eat. Oh, by the way, a pinch is about ¼ teaspoon and a dash is about ½ teaspoon (I made that up, but if you need a reference for amounts, use that).

If some of the first few recipes seem wordy, don't worry. They are not complicated. I am just giving you the play by play so you don't miss anything. The farther you go in the book, the less wordy I get. I'm assuming by the next few chapters, you'll get better at finding your way around the kitchen.

I have included a difficulty rating with each dish. The scale is 1 chef hat to 5 chef hats, with 1 chef hat being the easiest and 5 chef hats being the most difficult. I think you'll find that even the 5 chef hats meals are not too difficult to make, they just require a little more prep time.

Don Alexander

Quick and Easy Meals for One or Two People

Chapter Four

Pasta Dishes

Don Alexander

Quick and Easy Meals for One or Two People

Chili Mac:

Ingredients: 1 cup of elbow macaroni

Difficulty: ¼ lb. of ground beef or ground turkey

¼ cup of chopped onions

Paste Sauce (This is up to you how much. If you like a lot of sauce put a lot in. For one person, around ¾ of a cup should be enough).

1 tablespoon oil

A dash of garlic powder

A pinch of salt

A pinch of pepper

Boil the elbow macaroni according to the directions and times on the box (should be about 7-10 minutes). While the macaroni is boiling, add the oil to a saucepan and heat over medium heat for about 1 minute. Start browning the ground beef in the saucepan over medium to medium-high heat*. After about 2 minutes, add the onions, salt, pepper, and garlic powder.

After the ground beef is browned, (approximately 5 minutes), drain the fat. If you use ground turkey you should not have to drain it. There should be hardly any fat to drain. After draining the meat, return it to the stove. Add the pasta sauce to it and let cook over low heat for about 3 minutes stirring occasionally.

When the macaroni is finished cooking, drain it well and add it to the ground beef and pasta sauce. Mix it up, and you have chili mac. I like to add a little hot sauce to mine.

Another way to make this dish is to substitute sloppy joe sauce for the pasta sauce. This is pretty darn good too.

There are a couple of garlic bread recipes in Chapter 11, Side Dishes and Sauces, that go well with these pasta dishes.

*If the ground beef is frozen, start browning it on low. When the ground beef is thawed, turn up the heat to begin browning it, and then add the other ingredients.

Don Alexander

Quick and Easy Meals for One or Two People

Baked Cheese Spaghetti:

Ingredients:
Difficulty:

Spaghetti (however much you want) a good round handful is probably good enough.
Pasta Sauce (I would suggest something with meat and mushrooms already in it if you want meat in your sauce)
½ cup of mozzarella cheese
2 – 3 dashes of Parmesan cheese
A pinch of salt and pepper each

Boil the spaghetti until almost done. It will finish cooking in the oven. You can tell that it is almost done by tasting it. It should be limp, but still a little chewy. Drain the spaghetti well.

Off of the stove mix the spaghetti in with the pasta sauce (Again, however much sauce you like). Around 1 – 1 ½ cups of sauce should be good. Add in the salt, pepper, and mozzarella cheese. Put the mixture into a dish that can go in the oven. Sprinkle the parmesan cheese on top.

Preheat the oven to 350 degrees. Bake in the over at 350 degrees for about 10 minutes.

Don Alexander

Mostacolli:

Ingredients:	1 cup of mostacolli noodles
Difficulty:	¼ lb. of ground beef or ground turkey

¼ cup of chopped onions
Pasta Sauce (This is up to you how much. If you like a lot of sauce put a lot in. For two people, around 1 ½ cups should be enough).
1 tablespoon oil
A dash of Oregano
A pinch of salt
A pinch of pepper

This one is a lot like the chili mac with a twist.

Boil the mostacolli according to the directions and times on the box (should be about 7-10 minutes). While the mostacolli is boiling, add the oil to a saucepan and heat over medium heat for about 1 minute. Start browning the ground beef in the saucepan over medium to medium-high heat*. After about 2 minutes, add the onions, salt, pepper, and garlic powder.

After the ground beef is browned, (approximately 5 minutes), drain the fat from the saucepan. If you use ground turkey you should not have to drain it. There should be hardly any fat to drain. After draining the meat, return it to the stove. Add the pasta sauce to it and let cook over low heat for about 3 minutes, stirring occasionally.

When the mostacolli is finished cooking, drain it well and add it to the ground beef and pasta sauce. Mix it up, and you have mostacolli.

Another spin to this dish is to pour the finished mostacolli into a baking dish (preferably a glass baking dish). Put some shredded mozzarella cheese and some Parmesan cheese on top, and bake at 350 degrees for about 10 minutes.

*If the ground beef is frozen, start browning it on low. When the ground beef is thawed, turn up the heat to begin browning it, and then add the other ingredients.

Quick and Easy Meals for One or Two People

Fettuccini Alfredo:

Ingredients:
Difficulty:

Dried or fresh Fettuccini pasta. How much depends on how hungry you are. There will be enough sauce for two people if needed.
4 ounces of cream cheese (cubed)
¼ cup of grated Parmesan cheese (Fresh is best, but the can stuff works too)
¼ cup of milk
2 tablespoons of margarine

In whatever size pot will hold the amount of fettuccine you are going to cook, start boiling water. Remember, the fettuccine is going to expand while it cooks, so make sure you have enough room in the pot. Boil the fettuccine per the instructions on the package.

About 5 minutes before the fettuccine is done boiling start preparing the Alfredo sauce. In a medium to large saucepan, add the cream cheese, parmesan cheese, milk, and margarine. Stir all the ingredients in the saucepan over low heat. Continue stirring until the sauce is smooth.

Next thing to do is grab a plate and chow down. This dish is also a good dish for a date. If you are going to use this one for a date, I suggest a nice dinner salad and some garlic bread for appetizers. Remember, easy on the garlic bread if this for a date. You don't want your breath to make your date run for the door.

**Hint: Add a little salt of olive oil to the water to keep the pasta from sticking together.

Don Alexander

Quick and Easy Meals for One or Two People

Chapter Five

Rice Dishes

Don Alexander

Quick and Easy Meals for One or Two People

Fried Rice:
Ingredients:
Difficulty:

¼-½ lb of chicken or pork (Cut into small pieces)

1 cup of white rice
1 can of chicken broth (any grocery store has them)
3 tbsp of soy sauce
1 small onion chopped
1 stalk of celery chopped
2 tbsp of vegetable oil
1 egg beaten
1 small carrot chopped into small pieces

In a large skillet, fry the chicken in the oil at medium to high heat until the meat is almost cooked. Add the celery, onions and carrots, lower heat and cook until vegetables are slightly soft.

Add rice, and stir constantly until the rice has browned. Add the chicken broth and soy sauce. The broth should cover the rice and meat. If not add water until it does. Cover the skillet, turn the heat to low and cook until the broth is absorbed by the rice, and the rice is tender. If needed add water until the rice is tender. Once the rice is tender, move the rice to the side and make a hole in the center of the skillet.

Pour in the egg and scramble. When the egg is done, stir it into the rice.

Don Alexander

Rice and Italian Sausage:

Ingredients:
Difficulty:

1 can of Red Gold Italian tomatoes
1 cup water
½ cup rice
1-2 Italian Sausages sliced in to ½ inch pieces
A pinch of salt
A pinch of pepper

In a medium saucepan, bring the water to a boil. Add the rice, tomatoes, salt, pepper, and Italian Sausage. Bring the water to a boil again. Reduce the heat and cover. Let it simmer for about 15-20 minutes, or until the rice is cooked thoroughly. Stir occasionally to keep the rice on the bottom of the saucepan from burning. Add additional water if needed during cooking.

Quick and Easy Meals for One or Two People

Don Alexander

Apple and Brown Rice Pilaf:

Ingredients: ¼ cup of minced onion

Difficulty: 1 tablespoon of oil, preferable vegetable oil

¾ cup of white rice

¾ cup of chicken broth

A dash of thyme

A dash of pepper

1 medium apple, cored, peeled and diced. (Red delicious apples work well for this.)

A dash of parsley, dried or fresh.

Sauté the onions in oil in a non-stick frying pan until tender. Stir in the rice and brown slightly. Stir in the broth, thyme, and pepper. Bring this to a boil.

Cover the pan with a lid and reduce the heat. Simmer this for 15 minutes. Remove the pan from the heat. Stir in the apples and the parsley.

This dish is good both hot and cold.

Quick and Easy Meals for One or Two People

Chapter Six

Meat Dishes

Don Alexander

Quick and Easy Meals for One or Two People

Tater Tot Casserole:

Ingredients: ¼-½ of ground beef or ground turkey
Difficulty: ¼ cup of onions, diced

1 cup of frozen mixed vegetables
½ (10 ¾ ounce) can of cream of chicken
soup you can store the other half in an
air tight bowl in the fridge.
1 lb bag of frozen tater tots. Only use
¼-½ of the bag

Preheat oven to 375 degrees. Spray small glass baking dish with cooking spray. (If you do not have a glass baking dish, you can use a small aluminum baking pan).

Spread hamburger into the bottom of the pan. Make sure the entire bottom of the pan is covered. Sprinkle the diced onions over the ground meat. Sprinkle with a dash of salt and pepper.

Spread the frozen vegetables over the Ground meat and onions. Spread the soup with a spatula over the entire contents of the pan (make sure you take the soup directly from the can. Do not mix the soup with water.) Layer the tater tots on top of the soup, covering the entire top with the tater tots.

Bake at 375 for 45 minutes, or until the hamburger is done. Make sure to check the dish about a half an hour into cooking. If the tater tots are getting too brown, turn the oven down to 350 and cook for the next 15 minutes.

I like to eat this one with a little ketchup or hot sauce on top of it.

Don Alexander

Taco Bake:

Ingredients: ¼-½ of ground beef or ground turkey
Difficulty: ½ (1.25 ounce) package of taco
seasoning
½ cup of refried beans
½ cup of salsa
½ cup of shredded Monterey Jack
cheese

Preheat the oven to 325 degrees. Then, in a large skillet, brown the hamburger and drain the fat. Mix in the dry taco seasoning in the browned hamburger.

Spoon browned meat into a small glass baking dish. Spoon in a layer of refried beans over the meat and then do the same with the salsa.

Top the whole thing with the shredded cheese. Bake the dish at 350 degrees for about 20 to 25 minutes.

Quick and Easy Meals for One or Two People

BBQ Onion Cheeseburgers:

Ingredients:

Difficulty:

Estimate about ¼ lb of ground beef for each burger you want.

1 package of Lipton's Onion soup mix
Whatever barbecue sauce you like (I like Sweet Baby Ray's barbecue sauce)
A slice of American cheese for each burger
Hamburger buns or hard rolls
Lettuce, Tomato, Pickles and additional garnish as desired

In a large bowl, combine the ground beef and onion soup mix. Shape into hamburger patties. Fry hamburgers in a pan, or on a grill.

Cook for about 15 minutes, flipping over once half way through. About 1 minute before the burgers are done, brush the burgers with the barbecue sauce. Top the burgers with cheese.

Prepare the buns with the garnish. Put the burgers on the bun and enjoy.

Don Alexander

Quick and Easy Meals for One or Two People

Meatloaf:
Ingredients:
Difficulty:

½ lb of Ground Beef or Turkey
¼ cup of tomato juice
¼ cup of rolled oats
1 egg
¼ cup of chopped onion
A dash of salt
A dash of pepper
A couple of dashes of wochestishire sauce

Preheat oven to 350 degrees. In a large bowl, combine the ground beef (turkey), tomato juice, oats, egg, chopped onion, salt, pepper, and Worcestershire sauce. Mix thoroughly.

Mound the meat on a cookie sheet and form in to a loaf.

Bake for about 45 minutes, or until the meat is cooked thoroughly and the juices run clear. Let the meatloaf stand for about 5 minutes before cutting it.

If you would like some mashed potatoes to go along with your meat loaf, there are some good instant brands of mashed potatoes out there. You can also find good jarred gravy that goes good with both the meatloaf and mashed potatoes.

This meatloaf is great the next day for meatloaf sandwiches.

Don Alexander

Beef Stroganoff:

Ingredients:
Difficulty:

¼ lb of Ground Beef or Turkey
½ can of cream of mushroom soup
¼ cup of onions
¼ cup of water
Garlic powder
A dash of Pepper
A dash of Salt
Noodles (Egg Noodles work good for this)

Start boiling the noodles. Brown the ground beef or turkey and the onions. Drain the fat. Add the cream of mushroom soup and water. Add the garlic powder and a couple of dashes of pepper and salt, and cook until hot. Drain the noodles and pour the ground beef over the noodles to make a nice hearty meal.

Quick and Easy Meals for One or Two People

Beefy Eggs:

Ingredients:
Difficulty:

¼ lb. Of ground beef

1 egg

A pinch of salt

A pinch of pepper

A dash of garlic powder

A dash of oregano

In a frying pan, brown the ground beef. While the meat is cooking, beat the egg. Drain the fat out of the meat, and add the salt, pepper, garlic powder, and oregano. Dump the egg mixture in with the meat. Stir and cook until the eggs are done.

This may seem like a breakfast dish, but it makes a nice dinner also.

To make a sandwich out of this, toast some bread and put the beefy eggs on the toast.

Don Alexander

BBQ Beef and Rice:

Ingredients:
Difficulty:

¼-½ lb. Of ground beef
¼ cup of chopped onion
1 cup of water
½ cup of Barbecue Sauce
½ cup of instant white rice, uncooked
½ cup of shredded cheddar cheese
A pinch of salt
A pinch of pepper

In a medium size frying pan, brown the ground beef and onion. After the meat is cooked, drain the fat. Add the water and barbecue sauce to the pan. Bring to a boil. Stir in the rice turn the heat to low and cover the pan. Cook on low heat for 5-10 minutes, or until the rice is fully cooked. Sprinkle with the cheese and serve.

Quick and Easy Meals for One or Two People

Don Alexander

Beef and Corn Casserole:

Ingredients: ½ lb of ground beef
Difficulty: 1 tablespoon of vegetable oil

¼ cup of onion, chopped
½ cup of frozen corn
1 small, firm, ripe tomato, chopped
A pinch of salt
A pinch of pepper
½ cup of breadcrumbs

Heat the oil in a frying pan. Add the onion and pepper and cook until soft. Add the ground beef and cook until the beef is browned. Drain the fat.

Stir in the corn and salt. Put in a baking disk, cover with the tomatoes and sprinkle with the breadcrumbs.

Bake at 350 degrees until the breadcrumbs are brown, about 25-30 minutes.

Quick and Easy Meals for One or Two People

Burger Dogs:
Ingredients:
Difficulty:

¼ lb of ground beef
¼ cup of finely chopped onion
1 teaspoon of brown mustard
A pinch of salt
A pinch of pepper
4-5 slices of bacon
Hot dog buns

Mix together in a bowl the ground beef, onion, mustard, salt, and pepper. Roll the mixture into the shape of hot dogs. This should make 2-3 dogs. Wrap the burger dogs with the bacon in a spiral fashion.

Place the burger dogs on a baking sheet and broil in the over until the dogs are done how you like. About 12-15 minutes for medium.

Serve in the hot dog buns with your favorite condiments.

Don Alexander

Quick and Easy Meals for One or Two People

Chapter Seven

Chicken Dishes

Don Alexander

Quick and Easy Meals for One or Two People

Glazed Microwave Chicken:

Ingredients:

Difficulty:

2 Chicken Breasts (Boneless, skinless)
1 teaspoon of paprika
4 thin slices of lemon
2 tablespoons of honey
2 tablespoons of spicy brown mustard
A pinch of onion powder
½ teaspoon of lemon juice
½ teaspoon of curry powder

Sprinkle the chicken breasts with the paprika. Place 2 lemon slices on each chicken breast, and place the chicken breasts in a microwave dish. Cover loosely with wax paper and microwave for about 8-10 minutes (depending on the size of the chicken breasts). Make sure to turn the dish a half turn half way through cooking.

In a small microwave bowl, mix together honey, mustard, onion powder, lemon juice and curry powder. When the chicken is done, remove the chicken to a microwave-safe serving dish (just remove the chicken, and leave any liquid). Let the chicken sit while the sauce is cooking.

Microwave the honey-mustard sauce for 2 minutes. Spoon sauce over the chicken and microwave again for about 2 minutes, or until the glaze is hot and a fork can be inserted into the chicken with ease.

This one is good with a rice side dish.

Don Alexander

Honey Mustard Chicken:

Ingredients:
Difficulty:

2 Chicken Breasts (Boneless, skinless)
1/3 cup of Dijon mustard
1/3 cup of honey
1 tablespoon of dried dill (This is optional)
1 teaspoon of grated orange peel (You can buy this in the spice section of the grocery store, or you can grate your own orange peel)

Preheat the oven to 400 degrees. Combine the mustard and honey in a small bowl. Stir in the dill and orange peel. Line a baking sheet with aluminum foil. Place the chicken on the baking sheet. Brush the chicken with the honey mustard mixture. Place the chicken in the oven.

Bake for 15 minutes and then brush some more of the honey mustard mixture on the chicken. Bake for 15 minutes more. (30 minutes total baking time.)

This one makes a nice date dish also.

Quick and Easy Meals for One or Two People

Don Alexander

Stir Fry:
Ingredients:
Difficulty:

1 cup of mixed vegetables, frozen is fine

1 boneless, skinless chicken breast cut into strips
A pinch of pepper
A dash of garlic powder
Soy sauce, about ¼ cup
½ cup of white rice (or if you like brown rice, use that) Minute rice is fine. If using minute rice, cook the rice using the instructions on the box
2 tablespoons of oil (I like to use olive oil, but you can use vegetable oil if you want)

If using frozen vegetables, thaw them in a colander under hot water. Let the vegetables dry. Start boiling the rice in 1 – ½ cups of water. Bring the rice to a boil (uncovered), and then turn the heat down, cover with a lid, and simmer the rice for about 15 minutes.

When there is about 5 minutes left before the rice is done, do the following. Put a frying pan over med-high heat. Add the oil. Let the oil heat up for about 15-20 seconds.

Add the chicken to the frying pan. Stir the chicken for about a minute. Add the vegetables to the frying pan, stirring the whole thing often.

Add the pepper, garlic powder, and soy sauce. Keep stirring the vegetables for about 4 minutes.

Remove the rice from the stove. Drain the rice. Plate the rice first, and then pour the vegetables over the rice.

Quick and Easy Meals for One or Two People

Chicken Parmesan:
Ingredients:
Difficulty:

1-2 Chicken Breasts (Boneless, skinless)

A dash of salt

A pinch of pepper

1 egg

¼ cup of milk

1 cup of bread crumbs

1 cup (roughly) of pasta sauce

¼ cup of dried parmesan cheese

½ cup of shredded mozzarella cheese

Pasta of your choice (spaghetti, linguini, rotini)

In a bowl, mix the egg and the milk. This is going to hold the bread crumbs on the chicken. Sprinkle the bread crumbs, salt and pepper on a plate.

Dip the chicken in the egg and milk mixture, and then place them in the bread crumbs. Make sure that the whole chicken breast gets coated with the bread crumbs.

Place the chicken breasts on an oven safe sheet and cook at 350 degrees for 25 minutes. 7 –10 minutes before the chicken is done, heat up the pasta sauce in a sauce pan, and boil the pasta.

Drain the pasta, and put it on the plate. Place the chicken breast on the pasta. Sprinkle the chicken with the mozzarella cheese. Pour the pasta sauce over everything. Then sprinkle the parmesan cheese over the chicken and the pasta if you like.

Don Alexander

Caramelized Garlic Chicken:

Ingredients:
Difficulty:

1-2 Chicken Breasts (Boneless, skinless)

1 teaspoon of olive oil
2 garlic clove, minced
2 tablespoons of brown sugar

Heat the oven to 500 degrees. Line a baking pan with foil. Spray the foil with nonstick cooking spray. Heat the oil in a frying pan over medium heat until hot. Add the garlic, and cook for about 1-2 minutes or until the garlic begins to soften. Remove the garlic form the heat. Stir in the brown sugar until well mixed.

Place the chicken breasts on the baking pan. Spread the garlic mixture evenly over the chicken. Bake at 500 degrees for 10-15 minutes or until the chicken is fork tender and the juices run clear.

Quick and Easy Meals for One or Two People

Don Alexander

Cheesy Chicken and Broccoli Macaroni:

Ingredients:
Difficulty:

1-2 Chicken Breasts (Boneless, skinless), cut into small pieces
1 cup of chicken broth
1 cup of elbow macaroni, uncooked
1 cup of Velveeta cheese, cut up
1 cup of frozen chopped broccoli, thawed
A pinch of salt
A pinch of pepper

Spray a large frying pan with nonstick cooking spray. Turn the heat up to medium-high. Add the chicken and cook for 3 minutes or until no longer pink.

Stir in the broth. Bring to a boil. Stir in the macaroni. Reduce the heat to medium-low. Cover the pan with a lid. Simmer for 8-10 minutes, or until the macaroni is tender.

Add the Velveeta and broccoli. Stir until the Velveeta is melted. If you like your broccoli a little more tender, then microwave it for 1 minute before you add it to the pan.

Quick and Easy Meals for One or Two People

Cheesy Chicken and Vegetable Rice:

Ingredients:
Difficulty:

1-2 Chicken Breasts (Boneless, skinless), cut into pieces
1 cup of chicken broth
½ cup of quick cooking white rice (It may say Instant Rice on the package)
1 cup of frozen vegetable blend, thawed
1 cup of Velveeta cheese, cut up

Spray a large frying pan with nonstick cooking spray. Turn the heat up to medium-high. Add the chicken and cook for 3 minutes or until no longer pink.

Stir in the broth. Bring to a boil. Stir in the rice, vegetables, and Velveeta. Reduce the heat to medium-low. Cover the pan with a lid. Simmer for 5 minutes.

This one is just like the Cheesy Chicken and Broccoli one with a little twist.

Don Alexander

Honey Chicken Salad:

Ingredients:
Difficulty:

1 Chicken Breast (Boneless, skinless), cut into long strips about ½ inch thick
1 bag of ready mix salad. They sell several different kinds, but I like the ones with the different kinds of greens in them.
1 tablespoon of brown mustard
1 tablespoon of honey
½ cup of white wine
1 tablespoon of olive oil
A dash of salt
A dash of pepper

Put a medium sized frying pan on medium-high heat. Add the oil to the pan. In a small bowl, mix together the brown mustard, honey, wine, salt and pepper.

When the oil is hot, add the chicken. Stir to kind of coat the chicken with the oil so it doesn't stick to the pan. Pour the wine mixture over the chicken, and stir until all of the chicken is coated.

Cook and stir for about 4 minutes, of until the chicken is no longer pink. Take the pan off the heat and let sit for 5 minutes to cool some. While the chicken is cooling, open the ready mix salad bag and put some on a plate.

Top the salad with the chicken. You can also top the salad with your favorite salad dressing, and any other topping you like on a salad.

I like to top the whole dish with freshly grated parmesan cheese.

Quick and Easy Meals for One or Two People

Chicken Burritos:

Ingredients:
Difficulty:

1 Chicken Breast (Boneless, skinless), cut into long strips about ½ inch thick
1 tablespoon of chili powder
1 tablespoon of vegetable oil
¼ cup of refried beans
1-2 (10 inch) flour tortillas
1 cup of shredded cheese
1 cup of shredded lettuce
1 cup of chopped tomato

In a medium bowl, combine the chicken strips and the chili powder. Toss to coat the chicken evenly.

Heat the oil in a medium frying pan over medium heat until hot.

Add the chicken. Cook and stir for 4 to 5 minutes or until the chicken is no longer pink.

Add the refried beans and cook for 2 minutes, or until the mixture is hot, stirring frequently.

Spoon about 1/3 cup of the chicken mixture onto each tortilla. Top each tortilla with some cheese, lettuce, and tomato.

Fold into a burrito shape, and serve with your favorite salsa and sour cream.

Don Alexander

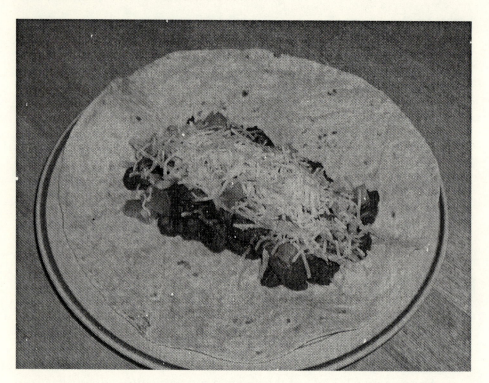

Quick and Easy Meals for One or Two People

Chicken Caesar Pita:
Ingredients:
Difficulty:

1 boneless, skinless chicken breast, cut into
long strips about ½ inch thick
1 cup of Torn romaine lettuce
1 tablespoon of oil
1 tablespoon of grated Parmesan Cheese
¼ cup Roasted Garlic Dressing
1 piece of Pita bread, cut in half

Heat the oil in a medium frying pan over medium heat until hot.

Add the chicken. Cook and stir for 4 to 5 minutes or until the chicken is no longer pink. Remove the chicken from the heat, and let cool for a couple of minutes.

In a medium bowl, mix the chicken, lettuce, cheese, and dressing.

Fill the pita bread halves with the chicken mixture, and enjoy.

These are great to take to work for lunch the next day if you make enough of them.

Don Alexander

Quick and Easy Meals for One or Two People

Chapter Eight

Pork Dishes

Don Alexander

Quick and Easy Meals for One or Two People

Crock Pot Pork Chops:

Ingredients:

Difficulty:

1-2 Pork Chops (I like the 1 inch thick pork chops with the bone still in them)
A pinch of salt
A pinch of pepper
A pinch of garlic powder
A pinch of onion powder
2 tablespoons of Olive Oil (I think that Olive Oil gives the best flavor, but you can use any kind of cooking oil)
1 can of Golden Mushroom Soup

Sprinkle each side of the pork chops with the salt, pepper, garlic powder and onion powder. Heat a large skillet on medium/high heat. Pour the olive oil in the heated skillet (Here is a good cooking tip: If you heat the pan up first before you put the oil in the pan, then the food will not usually stick to the pan when you brown it. Just remember: Hot pan, cold oil, food won't stick). I got this from the Yan can Cook show a long time ago.

Put the pork chops in the skillet and brown on each side for about 1 minute. Remove the pork chops from the skillet and place them in a crock pot.

Pour the can of Golden Mushroom soup in the crock pot. Put the lid on the crock pot and turn it on low for 8 hours.

The best way to do this for dinner is to get up 15 minutes earlier in the morning before work and prepare the chops. This way you have dinner waiting for you when you get home from work. Trust me, you'll be glad you got up those 15 minutes early when you taste this one.

I really like steamed green beans and mashed potatoes as sides for this dish. The sauce that is left in the crock pot makes great gravy for the potatoes.

Don Alexander

Quick and Easy Meals for One or Two People

Country Fried Pork:

Ingredients:
Difficulty:

1-2 Boneless, skinless Pork Chops (try to get the thin ones)

A pinch of salt
A pinch of pepper
A dash of onion powder
¼ cup of Olive Oil (I think that Olive Oil gives the best flavor, but you can use any kind of cooking oil)
1 cup of flour
2 tablespoons of baking powder
2-3 eggs

This one may sound difficult, but it's not. First you need to prepare the chops. You will need a paper (or regular) plate. Paper plates are just easier to clean up after. Dump the flour in the plate.

Sprinkle the salt, pepper baking powder and onion powder on the flour and mix it in. In a bowl, mix up the eggs like you would if you were making scrambled eggs.

Heat up the olive oil in a frying pan over medium heat. Check the oil to make sure it is the right temperature. You can do that by putting a drop of the egg mixture into the oil. If it starts to bubble a little bit, then the oil is ready. If not, then let the oil heat up some more. If it really crackles, then turn the heat down a bit.

Once the oil is heated, take a pork chop, dip it on to the plate with the flour mixture. Make sure you coat both sides with flour. Then dip the chop into the egg mixture making sure you coat both sides with the egg mixture. Then dip the chop back into the flour mixture, coating both sides. Why do you do this? Well, the first dip in the flour makes the egg wash stick to the chops, and the second dip in the flour mixture gives the chop the nice bubbly, crispy crust to it. That's why. Then put the chop into the oil. Do this with as many chops that you are going to make.

Cook the chop for about 4-5 minutes on each side, or until the outside of the chop has a nice brown coat on it.

Don Alexander

Monte Cristo Sandwich:

Ingredients:
Difficulty:

2 slices of thinly sliced, fully cooked ham per sandwich

a couple of ½ inch slices of bread (French bread or Vienna bread works good for this)
2 slices of Swiss cheese per sandwich
2 eggs
¼ cup of milk
2 tablespoons of butter

Place the slices of ham and cheese between 2 slices of bread. In a mixing bowl, beat together the eggs and milk.

Dip the sandwich in the egg mixture and turn it over. Make sure the bread soaks up the mixture (The same way you would make French toast).

Melt the butter in a skillet. Place the sandwich in the skillet and cook slowly, approximately 3-4 minutes on each side, or until each side is golden brown.

Quick and Easy Meals for One or Two People

Don Alexander

Quick and Easy Meals for One or Two People

Chapter Nine

Fish Dishes

Don Alexander

Quick and Easy Meals for One or Two People

Coconut Crusted Shrimp:

Ingredients:
Difficulty:

0 – 20 medium Shrimp (Depending on how hungry you, or the two of you are)
1 teaspoon of Garlic and herb seasoning
A dash of black pepper
¾ cup of flour
1-2 egg, well beaten
1 cup of shredded coconut

Preheat the oven to 400F. Spray a large baking sheet with nonstick spray (Pam, or whatever kind you like).

Sprinkle the garlic and herb seasoning and the pepper evenly over the shrimp. Place the flour, egg, and coconut in three small separate bowls. Now you are ready to start dipping.

Dip the shrimp first into the beaten egg, then into the flour, and then back into the beaten egg. Dip the shrimp into the coconut bowl, and coat it with the coconut. The double dipping of the egg will hold both the flour and the coconut on, and give you a nice crispy coating.

Place the shrimp on the baking sheet at least 1 inch apart from each other.

Bake the shrimp for about 12-15 minutes or until they are a golden brown and crisp.

If you like to get fancy, you can pick up some mango dipping sauce for this. It goes great with the shrimp.

Don Alexander

Quick and Easy Meals for One or Two People

Beer Battered Fried Catfish:

Ingredients:
Difficulty:

2 fillets of catfish (Frozen, un-battered fillets are fine. Just thaw them out first)
1 Cup flour
1 teaspoon baking powder
A dash teaspoon salt
1 tablespoon cooking oil (vegetable oil is fine)
1 Cup of beer (It usually works better if the beer is flat and at room temperature. I like darker beers for this one. It gives the batter more flavor).
1/2 tsp Tabasco sauce
1 inch of peanut oil in a skillet

It is best if you sift the flour into a medium bowl before you add the other ingredients to it. Add the baking powder and salt to the sifted flour in the bowl. Mix the tablespoon cooking oil, beer and Tabasco sauce in a small dish, and add to the flour mixture, stirring until smooth. Let the batter chill in the fridge for about a half hour.

In a skillet, heat the peanut oil to 375 degrees. If you don't have a thermometer, here's what you can do to test the oil to make it is the right temperature. Take a small drop of the batter, and drop it into the oil. It should start to bubble, and slowly turn brown. If it doesn't bubble, your oil is not hot enough. If it bubbles too much, and turns dark brown quickly, your oil is too hot. With practice, you'll get used to determining the temperature of oil.

Dip the cold strips of fish in the cold batter and cook in the hot oil for about 2-3 minutes on each side. After frying, drain the fish on some paper towels on a paper. This will drain some of the excess oil.

Deep fried fish is great with tartar sauce. If you don't have tartar sauce, here is an easy way to make some. Get a couple spoonfuls of mayonnaise, and one spoonful of some dill relish. Mix the two together. Trust me, it really works.

Don Alexander

Tuna Casserole:

Ingredients:
Difficulty:

1 8 oz can of tuna in water
1 10oz. can of cream of mushroom soup
1 cup of frozen peas (frozen green beans work also)
1-2 cups of dried rotini pasta noodles
A dash of salt
A dash of pepper
A dash of oregano
A dash of parsley flakes
½ cup of breadcrumbs
A dash of garlic powder
A dash of onion powder

Boil the pasta until it is almost done (just till it is still slightly chewy). Drain the pasta. Heat the peas in the microwave for 1 minute. Mix the pasta, tuna, cream of mushroom soup, peas, salt, pepper, oregano, and parsley in a bowl. Pour the mixture in a casserole dish. In a small bowl, mix the breadcrumbs, garlic powder, and onion powder. Pour the bread crumb mixture on top of the noodle mixture. Bake at 350 degrees for about 15 minutes.

This is great with hot sauce.

Quick and Easy Meals for One or Two People

Don Alexander

Quick and Easy Meals for One or Two People

Chapter Ten

Dinners for that Special Person

Don Alexander

Quick and Easy Meals for One or Two People

Since this book is designed for the single person, or for a couple without children, these recipes should come in handy. These are recipes that are designed to be easy to make, but look fancy. These dishes will make any date, girlfriend, or boyfriend feel like you really worked hard to make them a special dinner. Don't worry, these dishes are still easy, they just may take a little more effort than the ones in the previous chapters.

Don Alexander

Chicken Marsala:

Ingredients:
Difficulty:

2 Chicken Breasts (Boneless, skinless)
1 tablespoon of butter or margarine
A dash of salt
A dash of pepper
2-3 shallots diced (shallots are little pinkish looking onions)
1 cup of whole, fresh mushrooms
1 cup of Marsala wine
¼ cup of chicken stock or chicken broth (this comes in a can. You can put the rest in a freezer safe container and freeze it. Then you can just chip off and defrost what you need later)
A few dashes of parsley flakes (fresh parsley is better)
1 cup of cooked rice (minute rice is fine)

Salt and pepper the chicken on both sides. Melt the butter in a skillet. Brown the chicken breasts on both sides.

Add the chopped scallions, mushrooms, broth, and wine to the skillet.

Cover the skillet, reduce the heat to medium-low, and cook until the chicken is tender (this will take about 15 minutes).

Cook the rice while the chicken is cooking. The timing of when the rice is done will depend on whether or not you got instant rice. Regular rice takes about 15 minutes to make. Minute rice takes about 7 minutes.

Put the rice on the plate, and put the chicken on top of the rice. Spoon the sauce over the chicken and rice. Sprinkle the chicken with the parsley.

Note: For a thicker sauce, remove the chicken from the pan when done, turn the heat up to high, and reduce the liquid in the pan by ½.

Quick and Easy Meals for One or Two People

79

Don Alexander

Linguini and Chicken:

Ingredients:
Difficulty:

A handful of Linguini noodles

2 boneless skinless chicken breasts

Alfredo Sauce (You can find jars of pre-made Alfredo sauce). Or you can use the recipe in the Side Dishes and Sauces chapter.

1 tablespoon oil

A dash of oregano

A pinch of salt

A pinch of pepper

Boil the Linguini according to the directions and times on the box (should be about 7-10 minutes).

While the Linguini is boiling, add the oil to a frying pan and heat over medium heat for about 1 minute. Season the chicken on both sides with the salt, and pepper. Start frying the chicken in the frying pan over medium heat. After about 4 minutes, turn the chicken over, season that side of the chicken and cook for another 4 minutes.

After the chicken has cooked on both sides, remove it form the pan, and cut into it into inch slices.

When the Linguini is finished cooking, drain it well. Add 1 tbsp of oil into a frying pan and put it on medium heat. Add the Linguini to the pan and stir to lightly coat the Linguini with the oil (This will help keep the Linguini from sticking together). Add the Alfredo sauce, oregano, and the chicken to the pan. Cook over medium heat for a couple of minutes, until the sauce is hot.

Plate the Linguini and chicken, and enjoy.

There is a great garlic cheese recipe in the "Side Dishes and Deserts" section that would go great with this one.

Quick and Easy Meals for One or Two People

Potato Crusted Whitefish:

Ingredients:	A couple fillets of frozen white fish,
Difficulty:	thawed (cod, or
	what ever kind you want). Fresh fish
	would be best.
	1 or 2 medium potatoes
	A dash of salt
	A dash of pepper
	A dash of onion powder
	A dash of garlic powder
	½ cup of oil

Thaw the fish in a dish filled with milk. I know this sounds weird, but it will thaw the fish out and take away any fishy smell to the fish.

Peel the potatoes. Shred the potatoes with a hand shredder. You can even use frozen shredded hash browns, but they have to be fully thawed before you use them. Dry off the fish with a paper towel. This will let the potatoes stick to the fish better.

Heat the oil in a skillet. You will be able to tell that you have the right temperature by taking a piece of potato and dropping it into the oil. It should start to bubble and cook, but it should not bubble too much or burn quickly.

Take the shredded potatoes and form a coating around the fish until the entire fish is encased in shredded potato. Sprinkle the salt, pepper, onion powder, and garlic powder over the fish.

Set the fish into the frying pan and cook on each side for about 2-3 minutes, or until each side is golden brown. Remove the fish and set on a plate with paper towels on it to drain off the excess oil.

For a homemade tartar sauce, just take some dill relish and mix some mayonnaise in a dish.

This dish is good served with some rice and maybe some steamed vegetables.

Don Alexander

Chicken Cordon Blue:

Ingredients:
Difficulty:

A couple of boneless, skinless breasts of chicken (thawed if they are frozen)
2 slices of Prosciutto ham (1 slice per chicken breast)
2 slices of mozzarella cheese (1 slice per chicken breast)
1 cup of bread crumbs
A dash of salt
A dash of pepper

If you are using frozen chicken breasts, make sure that they are fully thawed. Pre-heat the oven to 350 degrees. Make a slice in the middle of the chicken breasts so that it opens like a book. Salt and pepper the chicken breasts. Put 1 slice of ham and 1 slice of cheese in each chicken breast and fold over like you are closing the book. Spread the bread crumbs on a plate. Coat the chicken on both sides with the bread crumbs. Place the chicken breasts in the pre-heated oven and cook for about 35-40 minutes.

For a fancier twist on this one, place 1 fresh spinach leaf inside each chicken breast with the ham and cheese.

Again, this goes good with a side of veggies and some rice. The garlic cheese bread is also good with this dish.

**There is a white wine sauce in the Side Dishes and Sauces chapter that will go good with this.

Quick and Easy Meals for One or Two People

Don Alexander

Stuffed Green Peppers:

Ingredients:
Difficulty:

2 Green Peppers
½ lb of ground beef
¼ cup of diced onions
¼ cup of white rice
A dash of salt
A dash of pepper
¼ cup of shredded cheddar cheese
1 can condensed tomato soup

Preheat the oven to 350 degrees. In a pot large enough to hold the 2 green peppers, bring enough water to cover the peppers to a boil.

Boil the green peppers for about 5 minutes. After the peppers have boiled for 5 minutes, remove them from the water and drain them.

In a skillet, brown the ground beef. Add the onion, salt, and pepper. Once the ground beef has browned, add 1 cup of water, the white rice and ½ of the can of tomato soup.

Stir the mixture until the soup is thoroughly mixed into the water. Cover and simmer for about 15 minutes. Most, if not all, of the liquid should be absorbed by the rice. Pour the mixture into a large bowl. Salt and pepper again.

Mix in the shredded cheese and stuff the mixture into the green peppers. Place the peppers into an over dish (preferably one with sides so any drippings will not spill onto the bottom of the over).

Mix the other half of the can of tomato soup with some water (just a couple of tablespoons full of water) and stir in a bowl to get it to a thick gravy consistency.

Spoon a couple of spoonfuls over each green pepper (you don't have to use all of the soup on the tops of the peppers). Bake for about 25 minutes.

Quick and Easy Meals for One or Two People

Lemon Pepper Chicken in a White Wine Sauce:

Ingredients:

Difficulty:

A couple of boneless, skinless breasts of chicken (thawed if they are frozen)
2 cups of white wine
2-3 shallots diced
2 tablespoons of butter
Lemon Pepper seasoning
A dash of salt
½ cup of heavy cream

If you are using frozen chicken breasts, make sure that they are fully thawed. Heat a frying pan over medium heat. Melt the butter in the pan. Sprinkle the salt and Lemon Pepper seasoning over the chicken. Add the chicken to the pan and cook for 2 minutes on each side.

Add the wine and shallots to the pan. Cover the pan with a lid, and turn the heat down to medium-low. Cook the chicken for about 10-15 minutes (depending on the size of the chicken breasts). Remove the chicken from the pan.

To make the sauce, leave the wine in the pan. Turn the heat up to medium-high. Let the wine reduce until it can fully coat the back of a spoon. Add the cream to the pan and cook for about 1 minute.

**If you will be making this for a date, a nice side dish would be some wild rice and steamed broccoli.

Don Alexander

Quick and Easy Meals for One or Two People

Chapter Eleven

Side Dishes and Sauces

Don Alexander

Quick and Easy Meals for One or Two People

Parsley Potatoes:

Ingredients: 3-5 medium red, potatoes (Depends on how many you want to make)
A dash of salt
A dash of pepper
A dash of garlic powder
A dash of onion powder
2 tablespoons of olive oil
¼ cup of dried parsley flakes (fresh parsley works better, but dried parsley flakes are good too)
¼ cup of grated Parmesan cheese

Wash, and boil the potatoes for about 10-15 minutes, or until you can stick a knife in them and they are soft. Let the potatoes cool a few minutes so you don't burn yourself when you cut them up. Cut the potatoes into chunks.

Heat up the olive oil on medium heat in a medium size skillet. Toss in the potatoes. Add the salt, pepper, onion powder, and garlic powder.

Toss the potatoes for about 1 minute. Add the parsley flakes, and toss the potatoes for about 1 minute or until they just start to lightly brown on the outside.

Remove from the heat, sprinkle the Parmesan cheese over the potatoes and enjoy.

Note: You can also microwave the potatoes instead of boiling them.

Don Alexander

Quick and Easy Meals for One or Two People

Grilled Asparagus:

Ingredients:

5-10 asparagus stalks (Depends on how many you want to make)
A dash of salt
A dash of pepper
Garlic Powder
Onion Powder
¼ cup of Olive Oil

Prep: Take a large Zip Lock freezer bag. Cut about 1 inch off of the bottom of the asparagus to get rid of the tough part. Wash the asparagus, and place them in the bag. Pour the Olive Oil in the bag with the asparagus. Add the salt, pepper, a dash or two of garlic powder and onion powder. Zip up the bag, and shake it up to make sure that all the Asparagus are coated. Place the bag in the fridge over night to let the Asparagus marinate. If you don't have the time to let the asparagus marinate overnight, 15 minutes marinating in the fridge should be enough.

Take the Asparagus out of the fridge about ½ hour before you are going to make them, and let them come up to room temperature in the bag. Throw them on the grill for about 5-8 minutes, and enjoy.

Don Alexander

Cheesy Garlic Bread:

Ingredients:

2-4 slices of any kind of bread you want. (French bread or Vienna bread works well for this.)
1-2 cups of shredded mozzarella cheese
Garlic Powder
Butter

Spread the butter on the slices of bread. Sprinkle the garlic powder over the buttered bread. You can put as much garlic powder on as you like. Sprinkle the cheese over the bread. Place the bread on a cookie sheet in the over. Turn the oven on Broil. Cook until the cheese is melted.

Quick and Easy Meals for One or Two People

Green Bean Casserole:

Ingredients: 1 can of French style green beans
1 small can of mushroom pieces & stems
1 small can of French fried onions
1 can of cream of mushroom soup
1 cup of grated cheddar cheese
A dash of ground pepper

Drain the liquid from the green beans and mushrooms. Mix the mushrooms, beans, soup, ½ of the can of onions and a couple of dashes of pepper in a bowl.

Cook in the microwave for 12 minutes.

Add the rest of the onions and the grated cheese on the top and cook for 2 minutes, or until the cheese is melted.

**This recipe makes enough for more than 2 people, so you will have some leftovers with this one. I included it in the book because it makes a great dish if you are hosting a diner party.

Don Alexander

Quick and Easy Meals for One or Two People

Garlic Sticks:

Ingredients:

1 package of frozen breadsticks
Olive Oil
Garlic Powder

Take 2-3 breadsticks out and place them on a baking sheet. While still frozen, brush the breadsticks with Olive oil. Sprinkle them with Garlic Powder. Bake per the instructions on the package.

Don Alexander

Alfredo Sauce:

Ingredients:

4 ounces of cream cheese
¼ cup of grated Parmesan cheese
¼ cup of milk
¼ cup of margarine

In a large saucepan, add all of the ingredients. Turn the heat on low. Stir the ingredients until the mixture is smooth

Quick and Easy Meals for One or Two People

White Wine Sauce:

Ingredients:
2 cups of white wine
½ cup of heavy cream
2-3 shallots minced
1 tablespoon of butter
A pinch of salt
A pinch of pepper

Heat a saucepan over medium heat. Add the butter and the shallots, salt and pepper. Sautee the shallots over medium heat for approximately 1 minute. Turn the heat on high and add the wine. Cook and stir occasionally until the wine reduces by about half. Stir in the cream, and cook for about 1 minute. The cream will thicken the sauce.

Don Alexander

About the Author

Don Alexander is not a professional chef. He is a 32 year old guy who just loves to cook. Don is a technology sales consultant who grew up in northwest Indiana. Don moved up to the northwest suburbs of Chicago after college, and has resided there since.

As a child, Don used to watch his mother cook for her 5 children. He was fascinated with the way she would prepare the food, cook it, and time everything just right so all the dishes were done at the same time.

Don's fascination with cooking hit a new level one day when his mother asked him if he'd like to stir one of the pots. Since that day, Don was hooked on cooking. His fascination with cooking even extended to watching cooking shows.

For the past 10 years Don has been making meals that he remembered from his childhood, from watching cooking shows, and meals he found in cookbooks. His only dilemma was that he was usually only cooking for himself, and all the meals he learned from his childhood, the cooking shows, and cookbooks made servings for 4 to 6 people. During these 10 years he has been taking what he has learned about cooking and designed quick and easy meals for 1 or 2 people.

His passion for cooking turned into the idea for a cookbook when he realized that there were thousands of people that were in his same situation. People who liked to cook, but didn't want the hassle of making large, complicated meals for just themselves, or just themselves and their significant other.

Don felt that the numerous quick and easy recipes for 1 or 2 people he had created for himself could benefit thousands of people. This is when he decided to write the book. Hopefully, this book will give an insight into Don's passion for cooking, and let people who have the same passion, but are only cooking for 1 or 2 people actually enjoy cooking. Hopefully this book will also let people who don't know how to cook be able to learn how to start cooking.

Printed in the United States
43901LVS00004B/3